C000017586

C000017586

JAMES DEAN™
IN HIS OWN WORDS

JAMES DEAN™
IN HIS OWN WORDS

Compiled by Neil Grant

CRESCENT BOOKS
NEW YORK • AVENEL, NEW JERSEY

EDITOR: JANICE ANDERSON, ART EDITOR: ROBIN WHITECROSS
PICTURE RESEARCH: EMILY HEDGES
PRODUCTION: CHERYL COOPER

THIS 1994 EDITION PUBLISHED BY CRESCENT BOOKS,
DISTRIBUTED BY OUTLET BOOK COMPANY, INC.,
A RANDOM HOUSE COMPANY,
40 ENGELHARD AVENUE, AVENEL, NEW JERSEY 07001

RANDOM HOUSE
NEW YORK • TORONTO • LONDON • SYDNEY • AUCKLAND

QUOTATIONS © 1991 JAMES DEAN FOUNDATION
UNDER LICENSE AUTHORIZED BY CURTIS MANAGEMENT GROUP,
INDIANAPOLIS, INDIANA, 46202 USA

COMPILATION AND DESIGN © 1991 REED INTERNATIONAL BOOKS LTD

ISBN 0 517 06101 5

8 7 6 5 4 3 2 1

PRINTED AND BOUND IN CHINA

CONTENTS

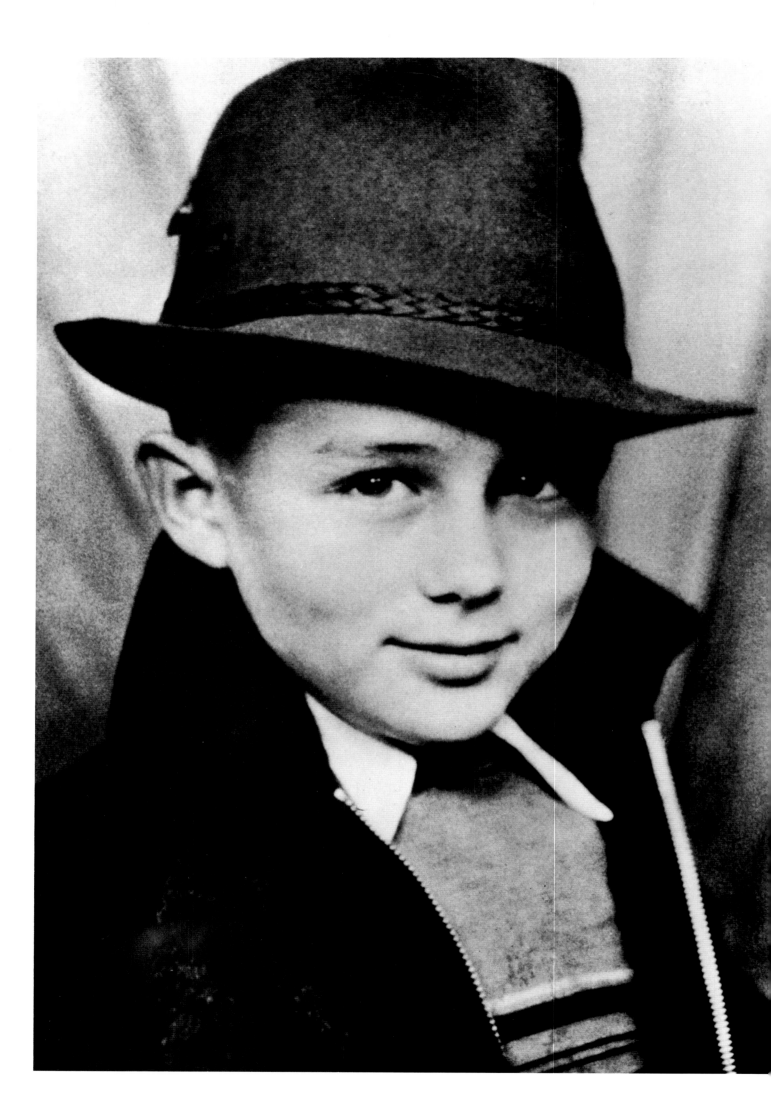

FARM BOY

*"My mother died when I was 9 years old…
What does she expect me to do? Do it all by myself"* (1955)

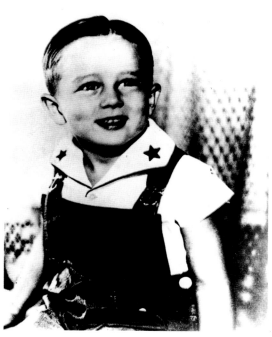

The death of James Dean at the age of 24 created a sensation and marked the start of a Jimmy Dean cult which, 35 years later, is still going strong. Not since the death of Valentino had the death of a film star provoked such hysterical scenes (there was a rock 'n' roll song called "James Dean's Christmas in Heaven"). Yet, when he died, this idol of America's youth had made just one film that had been seen by the general public (his second film, *Rebel Without A Cause*, was released within days of his death).

Jimmy Dean was a mixed-up young man who represented the growing discontent of suburban youth. He was really not so much an actor as a pop idol, like Elvis Presley. Girls went crazy over him; boys wanted to **be** him. Adults, naturally, were less impressed, and generally considered him a bad influence. Though he had some friends and supporters, especially older women, many of those who worked with him disliked him. As one producer said, "He was… the most exasperating young actor I ever worked with – slovenly, late, unspeakably detestable". But the same producer also said, of his work as an actor, "He was instinctively absolutely right."

He was born on 8 February 1931 in Marion, Indiana, and named James Byron Dean – though not (as he liked to imply) after the poet. His father, a dental technician, was a distant figure for whom the boy had little feeling. His mother was a gifted woman, utterly devoted to her only child. Her death when Jimmy was nine was a terrible disaster and probably explains at least some of his personality problems. Jimmy was brought up on a farm in Fairmount, Indiana, by an aunt and uncle, who were

"I was never a farmer.
I always wanted out of there..."

good to him – spoiled him in fact. At high school he was a success, good at games (despite being rather small and very short-sighted) and with a talent for drama which was encouraged by a teacher, Adeline Nall, the first of Jimmy's many mother-substitutes. In 1949 he won a local "dramatic-speaking" contest, characteristically choosing the Madman's monologue from *Pickwick Papers* and, equally characteristically, blaming Adeline Nall when he came only sixth in the national finals. Out of school, his interests were much like any other Mid-Western teenager. They included a love of speed; on his 18th birthday he was given his first motorcycle, a relatively harmless, Czech-made model.

Having graduated with prizes as top art student and best all-round athlete, he left for California, to study at Santa Monica College and to live with his father, now married again. Neither arrangement suited him, and the following year he transferred to UCLA to study theater and moved into an apart-

ment with his friend and future biographer, Bill Bast. "He was very, very stupid for a boy of his age," Bast wrote, "but there was also something quite strange about him." His savage extremes of mood, manic or depressive, made him a difficult friend and room mate.

Although he did not waste much time on other subjects, Jimmy certainly worked hard at drama, and not only in classes. He appeared in a UCLA production of *Macbeth*, playing Malcolm in what looks like a check tablecloth doubling as a kilt, in October 1950, and a few weeks later obtained his first professional job, through a Hollywood agent who saw promise in him. He was one of a group of teenagers in a Pepsi-Cola ad.

Early in 1951 he dropped out of college and started attending an acting workshop run by the actor James Whitmore, in imitation of the famous Actors Studio in New York, the home of "Method" acting. In March he had a small part in a TV play, *Hill Number One*, and some Los Angeles girls founded the first James Dean fan club.

8

"I used to sneak out of my uncles's house at night and go
to her grave and I used to cry on her grave-
'Mother, why did you leave me? Why did you leave me?
I need you'."

"I was **that** tall, and instead of doing little poems
about mice [at his aunt's Christian Temperance meetings],
I did things like 'The Terror of Death' - the goriest.
This made me strange -
a little harpie in short pants."

9

"[Athletics is] the heartbeat of every American boy,
[but] I think my life will be dedicated to art and dramatics."

"I've been riding (a motorcycle) since I was sixteen…
I used to ride to school…I used to go out for the cows on the
motorcycle. Scared the hell out of them.
They'd get to running and their udders would start swinging
and they'd lose a quart of milk."

"I have registered for summer and fall sessions at UCLA…
I am now a fully fledged member of the Miller Playhouse Theater
Guild Group…My knowledge of the stage and the
ability to design and paint sets won me the place of head stage
manager for the next production."

LETTER TO GRANDPARENTS (1949)

"It's a dream [being cast in the UCLA production of Macbeth].
Don't let anyone wake me up."

PROLOGUE TO GLORY

"I'm not the bobby-sox type and I'm not a romantic leading man.
They'll never give me a real chancel" (1951)

Jimmy's first TV appearance led nowhere. He became depressed and took to hanging out all night in disreputable places. Bill Bast moved out, leaving him to pay the rent alone; it hadn't been easy when there were two of them. Salvation of a sort came when Jimmy (who was bisexual) moved in with Rogers Brackett, a 35-year-old advertising man who also directed radio shows and had some film contacts, as a result of which Jimmy got a few bit-parts in movies, mostly non-speaking. This association also made it easier for him to dodge the draft on the grounds that he was homosexual. He added bull-fighting, bongo-playing and, later, photography to his hobbies.

In September 1951 he moved to New York. Brackett had been transferred there, and Whitmore (a theater man at heart) had recommended the move some time earlier.

New York suited him. He made some good friends, like Elizabeth "Dizzy" Sheridan, a dancer. They shared an apartment, which became a *menage à trois* when Bill Bast arrived from L.A. Jimmy also gained an agent, Jane Deacy, another mother-figure, who got him some small parts in TV plays, including *Prologue to Glory*, a long-forgotten offering of the *US Steel Hour*.

After long hesitation, he auditioned for the Actors Studio, a prime reason for going to New York. He and an actress named Christine Bell did a piece they had written themselves, and they were accepted – quite an achievement in itself. But, after only a few sessions, Jimmy gave up when he was bawled out by Lee Strasberg.

"To my way of thinking, an actor's course is set even before he's out of the cradle"

Months of poverty followed, interspersed by larks with Dizzy and Bill and others, bouts of depression, and endless visits to casting agencies. Rogers Brackett came to the rescue yet again: his contacts were responsible for Jimmy being cast in *See the Jaguar*, as a teenage boy who spends most of his life locked up. It was a fine part, but the play folded after four nights, in December 1952. Still, his reviews were good and Jimmy – and his friends – sensed that his career was beginning to roll. He began to get a lot of parts in TV (a medium he affected to despise), mostly as neurotic young men – dry runs for the parts he would pay in his three films. One of them, yet another version of the Jesse James story in which Jimmy was Bob Ford, gave him the chance to play with guns, which fascinated him. He also had a new 500 cc motorbike, which he wrote off, though without hurting himself, a year later.

Late in 1953 he finally landed another Broadway role, in *The Immoralist*, based on a novel by André Gide. He drove the producers and the director to distraction, turned in a brilliant performance, and gave his notice the night the play opened in New York. Elia Kazan, who had recently directed Marlon Brando's big successes (e.g. *A Streetcar Named Desire*), had been tipped off that Jimmy was a ringer for the part of Cal Trask in his forthcoming film, *East of Eden* – a part, incidentally, in which both Brando himself and Montgomery Clift, Jimmy's two great heroes, were interested. Kazan had seen Jimmy before at the Actors Studio, and wasn't much taken with him. He still wasn't, but he knew the moment the young man slouched sulkily into the room that here was Cal Trask.

In March, 1954, looking like a tramp and carrying his luggage in old shopping bags, James Dean returned to Hollywood.

"Those chairs (in agent's offices) are made scientifically
so that in exactly 11 minutes your backside begins to hurt.
But I beat the average. First I sit on one half of my fanny,
then on the other. They don't get rid of me until my 22 minutes are
up. But I'm beginning to take the shape of those chairs.
Maybe that's the shape of my destiny."

"I don't even want to be [just] the best. I want to grow so tall
that nobody can reach me. Not to prove anything,
but just to go where you ought to go when you devote your
whole life and all you are to one thing."

"I'm playing the damn bongo and
the world [can] go to hell."

"My purpose in life does not include
a hankering to charm society."

"An actor must learn all there is to know,
experience all there is to experience,
or approach that state as closely as possible."

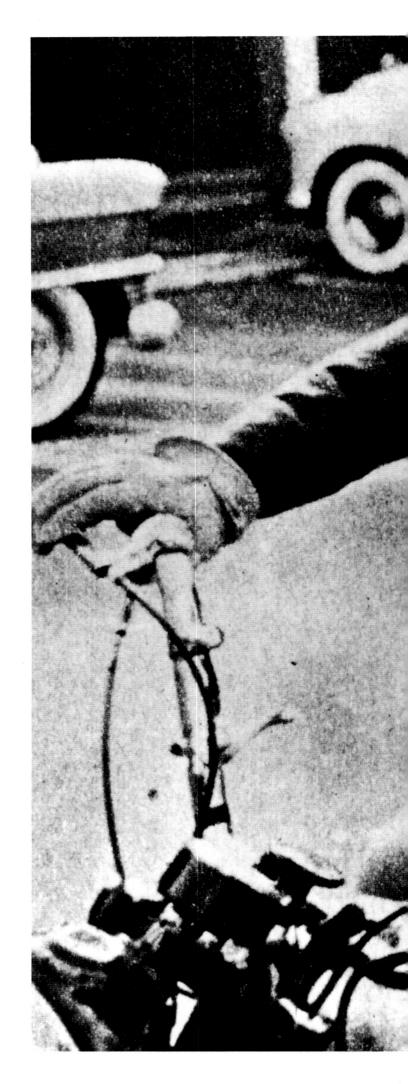

*"I've discovered a whole
new world here [in New York
City], a whole new way of
thinking…This town is the end.
It's talent that counts here.
You've got to stay with it or
get lost. I like it."*

*"New York's a fertile,
generous city if you can accept
the violence and decadence."*

20

"*If I let them [Strasberg and the Actors Studio] dissect me like a rabbit…then I might not be able to produce again*" (1953)

"*My neuroticism expresses itself in the dramatic. Why do most actors act? To express the fantasies in which they have involved themselves.*"

"*Rehearsals are quite confusing at this point. Lighting etc. Can't tell much about the show [**The Immoralist**] yet. Looks like a piece of shit to me.*"

LETTER TO A GIRLFRIEND (1953)

EAST OF EDEN

"No-one ever did anything for me.
I don't owe anything to anyone"

Elia Kazan specialized in young "discoveries" (though not all of them proved as successful as James Dean), and he understood Jimmy pretty well. He became something of a father, something of a personal manager, as well as a director. He even installed Jimmy in a live-in dressing room on the lot next to his own (his sleep was often disturbed as the walls were thin). But he was not blinded by Jimmy's faults, and nicknamed him "Creep".

Jimmy, remembering past failures, was resentful toward Hollywood and, as always, perfectly willing to offend anybody, especially anybody powerful or famous. He even antagonized Hedda Hopper, the formidable Hollywood gossip columnist, though she later became an admirer and defender. It was part of Jimmy's flawed emotional makeup that he felt he had to test anyone he – potentially – liked by behaving badly toward them. In *East of Eden* he was lucky to be cast opposite Julie Harris, an actress whose sweetness of character shines through her every performance, and who knew how to deal with Jimmy. His first approach was to offer to take her for a drive in his new MG, which he proceeded to drive dangerously fast. Julie had enough sense not ask him to slow down!

Others on the set were quickly antagonized. Jimmy's relationship with Raymond Massey, playing the father against whom Cal rebels though at the same time needing his love, was as prickly off-screen as it was on, though no doubt Kazan, one of the arch-priests of the Method, exploited this. "You never know what he's going to do," Massey

"I just want to make this picture and get back to New York" (MARCH 1954)

complained during filming "Make him read the lines the way they're written." Some hope!

Of course the part of Cal, alternately vicious and tender, was James Dean to a T, and those who knew him agreed with Kazan's feeling that Cal Trask **was** Jimmy – on the one hand "the lost, tormented, searching, gentle, enthusiastic little boy" (he was 23 but looks much, much younger in the film), on the other "the bitter, self-abusing, testing, vengeful monster". In spite of the fact that plenty of people involved with the film did not like him one bit, the months spent making *East of Eden* were probably among Jimmy's happiest times. All feuds and fury aside, he was part of a big family. At the end, when Julie Harris came to say goodbye to him, she found him in his dressing room crying like a small child and sobbing, "It's all over, it's all over." However, when the film opened in New York, with Marilyn Monroe handing out programs, Jimmy stayed away.

In the last stage of the filming, on the set at Burbank, Jimmy fell for a young actress working on the next lot, Pier Angeli. As a teenager she had given two or three incandescent performances in Italian movies and had been "imported" to Hollywood (where her unique magnetism soon disappeared under a thick layer of Hollywood conditioning). This was Jimmy's most serious affair. Like most people obsessed with themselves, Jimmy was probably not much interested in physical sex, and many of his relationships with girls were platonic (Carroll Baker, an actress who knew him near the end of his life thought "he died a virgin").

In October 1954 Pier told Jimmy she was going to marry Vic Damone, an oily crooner but of Italian background and a Roman Catholic. Jimmy broke up – one story says he hit her – and when the marriage took place next month, the vows were hard to hear above the noise of Jimmy revving up his motorbike outside the church. Pier's marriage ended messily four or five years later (probably a marriage to Jimmy wouldn't have lasted that long), and she committed suicide in 1971.

"I can't divert into being a social human being when
I'm working on a hero like Cal, who's essentially demonic."

"Have been telling everyone to fuck off, and that's no good.
I couldn't make them believe I was working on my part.
Poor Julie Harris doesn't know what to do with me.
Well to hell with her, she doesn't have to do anything to me."

LETTER TO NEW YORK GIRLFRIEND (APRIL, 1954)

*"I've told the girls
here to kiss my ass, and
what sterile, spineless,
stupid prostitutes they are...
I HAVEN'T BEEN
TO BED WITH NOBODY,
and won't until after
the picture and I am home
safe in New York City
(snuggly little town that is)."*

*"The best thing about being
a bachelor is that you can
get into bed from either side."*

28

"A new addition has been added to the Dean family.
I got a red '53 MG… My sex pours itself into fat curves,
broadslides and broodings, drags, etc.
You have plenty of competition. My motorcycle, my MG
and my girl. I have been sleeping
with my MG. We make it together, honey."

(LETTER TO NEW YORK GIRLFRIEND)

"I'm really kind and gentle.Things get mixed up all the time.
I see a person I would like to be very close to
(everybody) then I think it would be just the same as before
and they don't give a shit for me. Then I say
something nasty or nothing at all and walk away. The poor
person doesn't realize that I have decided I don't
like him. What's wrong with people?" (1954)

"I try so hard to make people reject me. Why?" LETTER (1954)

"Just an easy kind of friendly thing. I respect her. She's untouchable. We're members of totally different castes. You know, she's the kind of girl you put on a shelf and look at. Anyway, her old lady [Pier Angeli's mother] doesn't like me. Can't say I blame her."

"For better or for worse, I'm going to spend the rest of my days with her [Pier Angeli]"

REBEL WITHOUT A CAUSE

"Success is only in the mechanics of it.
All the rest I have because I'm me and I've got it all"

Rebel Without A Cause is a film about middle-class juvenile delinquency, a subject that caused a lot of concern in the America of the Fifties. It was an old Warner Bros idea, originally intended for Brando, which was resurrected by the director Nicholas Ray. After some trouble with the screenplay the project was approved and in January 1955 the studio announced that it would be made with James Dean starring as the near-psychotic hero, Jim Stark. (All Jimmy's characters seemed to have such brisk monosyllabic names, like his own, though he had once considered calling himself Byron Dean).

Jimmy was again lucky with his director. Nick Ray was a nonautocratic director, quite prepared to delay shooting an hour or so while Jimmy psyched himself up for a scene (Jim Backus, who played Jim's father, said that Dean virtually co-directed the film). Ray was also, like Jimmy, a Mid-Westerner, something of a rebel, and hostile to the

Hollywood establishment. Natalie Wood, playing Jim's girlfriend, was sisterly, like Julie Harris, but less of an equal (though, as a long-time child actress, more experienced in films). Sal Mineo, the hero's adoring side-kick, later admitted to adoring him as much off-set as in the film. Even more than *East of Eden*, *Rebel* gave Jimmy a family-like social setting in which he felt relatively comfortable. Because his immediate associates were on the whole more amenable, Jimmy too seems to have been often in a more kindly mood. Natalie Wood and Dennis Hopper (one of the juvenile gang), among others, later remarked on how helpful he was to them in a technical sense – something Raymond Massey would have found hard to believe.

Partly, no doubt, for lack of opportunity, Jimmy spent less time chasing girls or driving cars (his contract forbade motor racing during filming), and less time hanging

"I think all of us have a great need to let go. Acting is my outlet"

around with the slightly unsavory characters nicknamed "the Nightwatch" and, by one columnist, "the Creeps". A central figure in this company was a Finnish-born actress, Maila Nurmi, who had acquired some notoriety introducing TV horror movies in the character of "Vampira". Though she was at least ten years older than Jimmy, there was some gossip about an affair.

More productively, Jimmy acted in several TV plays, including a melodrama called *The Dark, Dark Hours* which also starred Ronald Reagan. Later, asked his opinion of Dean, Reagan characteristically remarked that he was surprised how much Dean the person resembled Dean the actor.

East of Eden opened in March 1955, and from that time until his death – a mere six months – Jimmy was a celebrity, the most talked-about star in the Hollywood firmament. Not every critic liked the movie; some hated it, and described Dean as a poor copy of Brando, but no one was indifferent to it, and raves predominated. Discussion of Jimmy's "technique" (Kazan said he had none, compared with Brando) was irrelevant, though many noticed how Jimmy, who always acted more with his body than with his voice, possessed an unusual degree of physical control.

Journalists and columnists now gathered around the Warner Bros lot like bees around a honey pot, and Jimmy was the Queen Bee. Two days after the *Eden* opening, a famous feature on Jimmy was published in *Life* magazine. The photos were painstakingly obtained over several weeks and many locations, nationwide, by Dennis Stock, who became one of Jimmy's most perceptive and observant friends, and was hired as "dialogue coach" by Nick Ray for *Rebel*. Most people, even Elia Kazan (though not Jimmy himself), were surprised by the sheer magnitude of Jimmy's success in *Eden*, and Warner Bros hastened to extend his contract. He started work on his next picture before filming of *Rebel* was finished.

"I put everything I had into that one,
and I'm pleased with the general result.
Any writer, musician, painter or actor will tell you
that when they look back on their work
they know it could be improved. But in the end you have to
say OK, that's it, it's finished — it stands or falls as it is.
I now regard Natalie [Wood], Nick [Ray] and Sal [Mineo] as
co-workers. I regard them as friends...
about the only friends I have in this town."

"What the hell are you [Nicholas Ray] doing?
Can't you see I'm having a real moment? Don't you ever cut
a scene when I'm having a real moment."

*"Don't **act**. If you're smoking a cigarette, smoke it.*
Don't act like you're smoking it."
To Dennis Hopper

"When you know there is something more to go in
a character, and you're not sure what it is, you just got to go
out after it. Walk on a tightrope."
To Dennis Hopper

41

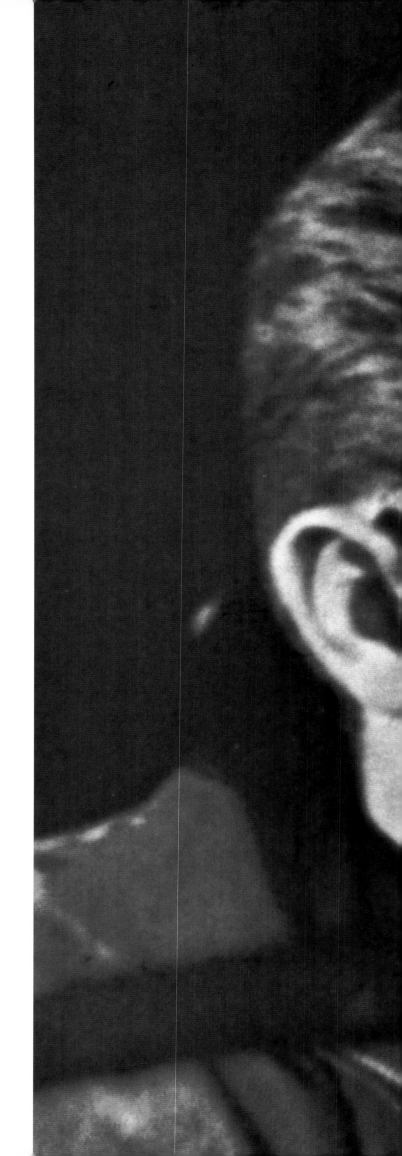

*"I went out and hung around
with kids in Los Angeles before
making the movie [**Rebel
Without a Cause**]… They
wear leather jackets, go
out looking for someone to
rough up a little. These aren't
poor kids, you know.
Lots of them have money,
grow up and become pillars
of the community.
Boy, they scared me!"*

*"People were telling me
I behaved like Brando
even before I knew who Brando
was. I'm not disturbed by
the comparison —
nor am I flattered"* (1955)

"*I don't care what people write about me. I'll talk to [reporters] I like. The others can print whatever they please.*"

"*What counts to the artist is performance, not publicity. Guys who don't know me, already they've typed me as an oddball.*"

"*I think the prime reason for existence, for living in this world is discovery.*"

44

"I'm a serious-minded and intense little devil —
terribly gauche and so tense that I don't see how people can
stay in the same room as me.
I know I couldn't tolerate myself."

"Whatever's inside making me what I am,
it's like film. Film only works in the dark. Tear it all open
and let in the light and you kill it."

"It's …just…that…I…am frightened. Frightened by this success.
It's all come too early for me."

GIANT

"I don't want to burn myself out…
I've made three pictures in the last two years"

Unlike Jimmy's previous pictures, *Giant* was a big Hollywood epic, in which he received equal billing with heavyweight Holly-wood stars Rock Hudson and Elizabeth Taylor, and it was directed by one of the top established Hollywood directors, George Stevens. To begin with, he was delighted with the prospect, but the styles of Dean and Stevens were thoroughly incompatible, and Stevens was irritated by Jimmy's view of the story, which put his own character, Jett Rink, at the centre, not to mention such behaviour as urinating, before his first scene with Liz Taylor, in front of a large crowd. Although Liz was fond of him – she was none too keen on Stevens herself – Jimmy didn't like Rock Hudson either. (The feeling was mutual: Dean "never smiled, was sulky and had

no manners", Hudson reported). This reflects the relationship of the characters they play. Jimmy's unique and uncanny identification with the role he was playing (for *Giant* he endlessly practiced a Texan accent and mastered difficult rope tricks) always affected his off-screen relationships. His chief chums were Dennis Hopper and a photographer, Sandy Roth, who, with his wife, became something like a substitute parent for Jimmy in his last months. But Jett Rink is a loner and, on and off the set, Jimmy was a bit of a loner too.

One of Stevens's diktats was that Jimmy should do no motor racing while the film was being made but, shortly before joining the company on location in May 1955, he took part in a race at Santa Barbara, failing

"There really isn't an opportunity for greatness in this world"

to finish the course. One professional driver judged that Jimmy, though talented, would not have made the top rank as a racing driver because he wouldn't take risks with other drivers, however careless of breaking his own neck.

On location near the Mexican border, the filming went fairly smoothly, but things deteriorated when the company returned to the Warner studios at Burbank. Jimmy was back among the Hollywood nightspots, conducting a stormy affair with continental sexpot Ursula Andress (one paper reported that Jimmy was learning German so he and Andress could carry on their quarrels in two languages), and he often arrived late on the set. One day he did not turn up at all, which caused a major row with George Stevens and kept the gossip writers busy for days.

At this time Jimmy met more of his childhood heroes, like Humphrey Bogart (Bogie, like Brando, was not much impressed), Gary Cooper and Alec Guiness, who, being shown Jimmy's new and more powerful Porsche, had a premonition of the young star's death a week later. Despite his bad reputation, there was talk of Jimmy forming

his own production company under the Warners umbrella, and he signed up for two TV dramas in New York – at fat fees. His last job was a film interview for an organization devoted to road safety.

As soon as *Giant* was finished, Jimmy's ambition was to get back on the track. He gave his cat, Marcus (a gift from Liz Taylor), to a girlfriend to look after and set off for a race in Salinas. Next to him in the 170-mph Porsche sat a mechanic, Rolf Wutherich, while Sandy Roth and another friend came along behind in Jimmy's station wagon. Near Bakersfield he was given a ticket for speeding, the officer telling him (or so he said later) that if he didn't slow down he would never reach Salinas alive. Toward sunset he collided at an intersection with a car driven by a 23-year-old student. Exactly whose fault it was is still uncertain. No doubt Jimmy was going too fast, and the other driver may have failed to see the dusty Porsche in the failing light until too late. Rolf Wutherich was thrown clear, the other driver suffered no major injuries, but Jimmy was dead within minutes.

His neck had been broken.

"The trouble with me is that I'm just dog tired.
Everybody hates me and thinks I'm a heel. They say I've gone
to Hollywood, but honestly I'm just the same as when
*I didn't have a dime. I'm tired. I went into **Giant** immediate...ly*
*after a long hard schedule in **Rebel**.*
Maybe I'd better just go away."

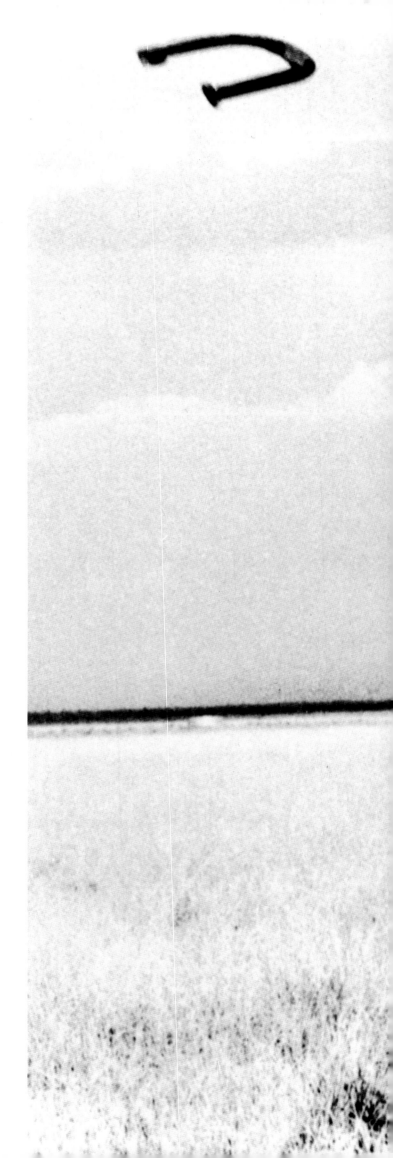

"I want to do **Hamlet** soon.
Only a young man can play him
as he was – with naivety.
Laurence Olivier played it
safe. Something is lost when the
older men play him.
They anticipate his answers.
You don't feel that Hamlet
is thinking – just declaiming."

"I practiced [**Hamlet**]
for years in the middle of a
wheatfield in Indiana."

*"We fight like cats and dogs – no, on second
thoughts, like two monsters. But then we make up and it's
fun. Ursula [Andress] doesn't take any
baloney from me and I don't take any baloney from her.
I guess it's because we are both egotistical."*

*"What the hell would she [Ursula Andress] have
in common with a poor farm boy? If it weren't that I was
up there on the screen, her and people like her
wouldn't give me the time of day."*

"Stevens has been horrible. I sat there for three days,
made up and ready to work at 9 o'clock every morning.
By 6 o'clock I hadn't had a scene or a rehearsal.
I sat there like a bump on a log watching that hog lumpy
Rock Hudson making love to Liz Taylor.
I'm not going to take it any more."

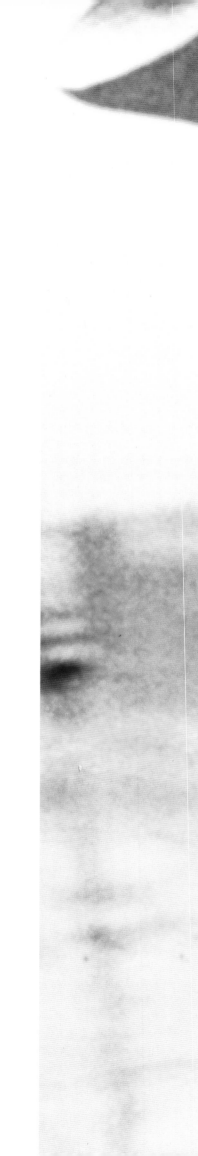

"I was so nervous...So I figured if I could piss in front of those 2,000 people, man, and I could be cool, I figured if I could do that, I could get in front of the camera and do just anything, anything at all."

"I'm a much better actor than what's being done with me at the moment. I'm being inhibited, I'm not able to exersize the full capacity of my abilities."

"I hate anything that limits progress and growth."

56

*"I want an airplane next –
don't write about that.
When things like that appear
in print, the things you love,
it makes you look like a whore."*

*"You know what a crazy
life I lead. I just figured, you
never know…I might go
out one night and never come
home. Then what would
happen to Marcus?"*

*"Racing is the only time
I feel whole"* (1955)

"My life story seems so dull to me that I can't really
tell it without the "Funeral March" or "Hearts and Flowers"
providing a mournful background" (1955)

"I've got a lot of growing up to do yet.
I've got to be given time to master the art of handling
Hollywood – to learn what to say and what not to say" (APRIL 1955)

I used to fly around quite a bit.
Took a lot of unnecessary chances on the highway.
Now I drive extra-cautious"
FILM INTERVIEW (SEPTEMBER 1955)

"I'm a small-town boy, with small-town ideas.
That's how I want to live.
I intend some day to retire and farm" (1955)

"The only greatness for a man is immortality" (1950)

"Live fast, die young
and have a good-looking corpse"
LINE FROM A NICHOLAS RAY MOVIE, QUOTED BY DEAN

"If I live to be a hundred,

there won't be time to do everything I want" (1955)

"Man, when you've got

to go you got to go. You don't just stop

to calculate the risk"

*"That guy's **got** to see us"*

<small>ALLEGED LAST WORDS</small>

PICTURE CREDITS

THE PUBLISHER WOULD LIKE TO ACKNOWLEDGE WARNER BROTHERS
FOR PHOTOGRAPHS RELATING TO *EAST OF EDEN* (WARNER BROTHERS, 1955), *REBEL WITHOUT A CAUSE*
(WARNER BROTHERS, 1955) AND *GIANT* (WARNER BROTHERS, 1956).

PAGE 1: James Dean: a late portrait. LONDON FEATURES INTERNATIONAL

PAGE 2: "James Dean: the story of the strangest legend since Valentino" said the caption by this picture on the cover of Look magazine, October 1956. TOPHAM PICTURE LIBRARY

PAGE 6: James Dean aged 8. THE KOBAL COLLECTION

PAGE 7: Four-year-old Jimmy had his hair well slicked down for this family portrait. AQUARIUS PICTURE LIBRARY

PAGE 8: Farm boy Jimmy Dean. THE KOBAL COLLECTION

PAGE 9: Already interested in high jumping as a boy, James Dean was to break the county pole vault record when he was 17. THE RONALD GRANT ARCHIVE

PAGE 10: James Dean, centre front, in the Fairmount High School baseball team. He was also in the Indiana school's football team. THE KOBAL COLLECTION

PAGE 11: The year he left high school. AQUARIUS PICTURE LIBRARY

PAGE 12: Hopeful young actor: this portfolio headshot of Jimmy, aged 21, was taken in New York. PICTORIAL PRESS

PAGE 13: As Malcolm in the UCLA Theater's production of "Macbeth", October 1950. PICTORIAL PRESS

PAGE 14: As Cal Trask in *East of Eden* (Warner Brothers, 1955). POPPERFOTO

PAGE 15: A dark polo-neck replaces the more familiar white T-shirt in this publicity shot. THE RONALD GRANT ARCHIVE

PAGE 16: Another picture promoting the James Dean image, this one from *c.* 1951. CAMERA PRESS

PAGE 17: Every movies hopeful must have his portfolio: this 1951 display of the many moods of James Dean was the work of Hollywood photographer Ray Millar. PICTORIAL PRESS

PAGE 18: This picture of Jimmy playing the bongo drums was used by Warner Brothers as a promotional postcard. AQUARIUS PICTURE LIBRARY

PAGE 19: Jimmy as matador; perhaps he has in mind one of his favorite books, Ernest Hemingway's bullfighting masterpiece, "Death in the Afternoon". AQUARIUS PICTURE LIBRARY

PAGE 20: James Dean left the West Coast to look for theater work in New York in September 1951. LONDON FEATURES INTERNATIONAL

PAGES 20–21: Quintessential teenage rebel: Jimmy Dean with leather jacket and motorbicycle. THE RONALD GRANT ARCHIVE

PAGE 22: With actress Pat Hardy in a 1955 TV drama, "The Unlighted Road". PICTORIAL PRESS

PAGE 23: As Bachir in the 1954 Broadway production of André Gide's "The Immoralist", which also starred Louis Jordan and Geraldine Page. CAMERA PRESS

PAGE 24: This publicity still was a favorite cover picture with magazine editors the world over. PICTORIAL PRESS

PAGE 25: Wardrobe test for Cal Trask in *East of Eden*. THE RONALD GRANT ARCHIVE

PAGE 26: With Julie Harris in *East of Eden*. THE KOBAL COLLECTION

PAGE 27: Railroad yard scene, *East of Eden*. THE RONALD GRANT ARCHIVE

PAGE 28: As Cal Trask, Jimmy does his own stunts in *East of Eden*. POPPERFOTO

PAGES 28-9: Moody moment with a recorder - an outshot from *East of Eden* LONDON FEATURES INTERNATIONAL

PAGE 30: In a fairground shooting gallery: *Rebel Without A Cause* (Warner Brothers, 1955). LONDON FEATURES INTERNATIONAL

PAGE 31: James Dean played a psychopath in the TV drama, "The Unlighted Road". AQUARIUS PICTURE LIBRARY

PAGE 32: James Dean finding the light "that shines on you alone" on the set of *East of Eden*. THE KOBAL COLLECTION

PAGE 33: Season's greetings, 1954. AQUARIUS PICTURE LIBRARY

PAGE 34-5: As Cal Trask in *East of Eden*. THE RONALD GRANT ARCHIVE

PAGE 35: With early love, Pier Angeli. TOPHAM PICTURE LIBRARY

PAGE 36: Moody pose for publicity. DENNIS STOCK, MAGNUM PHOTOS.

PAGE 37: A first screen kiss for Natalie Wood in *Rebel Without a Cause*. AQUARIUS PICTURE LIBRARY

PAGE 38: The young stars of *Rebel Without a Cause* ham it up for the camera. REX FEATURES

PAGE 39: Sal Mineo as Plato, James Dean as Jim Stark, and Natalie Wood as Judy in *Rebel Without a Cause*. THE KOBAL COLLECTION

PAGE 40: Archetypal teenage rebel: Dean in *Rebel Without a Cause*. THE KOBAL COLLECTION

PAGE 41: Shot from the opening scenes of *Rebel Without a Cause*, with Jim Stark still dressed as the boy "from a good family". THE KOBAL COLLECTION

PAGES 42-3: The rebel without a cause. REX FEATURES

PAGE 44: In the make-up department for *Rebel Without a Cause*. Is the bird offering advice on the chess problem? PICTORIAL PRESS

PAGES 44-5: Sometimes, movie-making is one big yawn… PICTORIAL PRESS

PAGE 46: A serious Dean, photographed by Phil Stern while visiting the back lot of *Guys and Dolls* in Hollywood in 1955. REX FEATURES

PAGE 47: Publicity portrait, 1955. DENNIS STOCK, MAGNUM PHOTOS.

PAGE 48: By now famous and a "bobby soxer idol", James Dean is photographed waiting to go in front of the cameras for *Giant* (Warner Brothers, 1956). REX FEATURES

PAGE 49: While filming *Giant*, Jimmy and a friend spent some time hunting in the surrounding countryside, until one day Jimmy decided he had had enough: rabbits and birds "don't do anybody any harm". AQUARIUS PICTURE LIBRARY

PAGE 50: Rest between takes, filming *Giant* in Marfa, Texas, 1955. LONDON FEATURES INTERNATIONAL

PAGE 51: Feeling close to being burnt out? When this picture was taken, James Dean had made three pictures in two years. THE RONALD GRANT ARCHIVE

PAGE 52: On location for *Giant*, 1955. LONDON FEATURES INTERNATIONAL

PAGES 52-3: Enjoying a local sport: throwing horseshoes while on location in Texas for *Giant*. PICTORIAL PRESS

PAGE 54: With Ursula Andress at the 1955 Academy Awards. PICTORIAL PRESS

PAGE 55: Wardrobe test for Jett Rink, the strike-it-rich oil man in *Giant*. REX FEATURES

PAGES 56-7: *Giant*. REX FEATURES

PAGES 58-9: A photograph by Sanford Roth of James Dean with his pet cat, Marcus, given him by Elizabeth Taylor.. THE RONALD GRANT ARCHIVE

PAGE 59: Sports cars and racing them were passions with Jimmy; "Out on the track I learn about people and myself". LONDON FEATURES INTERNATIONAL

PAGE 60: One of the last portraits of James Dean, 1955. THE KOBAL COLLECTION

PAGE 61: Studying the camera angles, on location for *Giant*. THE RONALD GRANT ARCHIVE

PAGE 62: James Dean's pride and joy. He bought this Porsche Spyder 550 the week before he died. Forbidden by his contract to race drive during the making of *Giant*, he was killed driving the car to a race meeting at Paso Robles, California, the weekend after filming was over. PICTORIAL PRESS

PAGE 63: The wrecked Porsche in which James Dean died, near Chalame, California, 30 September 1955. AQUARIUS PICTURE LIBRARY

ALTHOUGH EVERY EFFORT HAS BEEN MADE TO TRACE THE COPYRIGHT HOLDER, WE APOLOGISE IN ADVANCE FOR ANY UNINTENTIONAL OMISSIONS AND WOULD BE PLEASED TO INSERT THE APPROPRIATED ACKNOWLEDGEMENTS IN ANY SUBSEQUENT EDITION OF THIS PUBLICATION.